The

Insistence

of

Beauty

Also by Stephen Dunn

Poetry

Local Visitations
Different Hours
Loosestrife
New & Selected Poems, 1974–1994
Landscape at the End of the Century
Between Angels
Local Time
Not Dancing
Work and Love
A Circus of Needs
Full of Lust and Good Usage
Looking for Holes in the Ceiling

Prose

Walking Light: Essays & Memoirs
Riffs & Reciprocities

Chapbooks

Five Impersonations
Winter at the Caspian Sea (with Lawrence Raab)

The
Insistence
of
Beauty

p o e m s

Stephen Dunn

 W. W. Norton & Company   New York · London

For information about permission to reproduce selections from this book,
write to Permissions, W. W. Norton & Company, Inc.
500 Fifth Avenue, New York, NY 10110

Manufacturing by Courier Westford
Book design by Chris Welch
Production manager: Anna Oler

Library of Congress Cataloging-in-Publication Data
Dunn, Stephen, date.
The insistence of beauty : poems / Stephen Dunn.—1st ed.
p. cm.
ISBN 0-393-05955-3 (hardcover)
I. Title
PS3554.U49I57 2004
811'.54—dc22   2004013773

W. W. Norton & Company, Inc., 500 Fifth Avenue, New York, N.Y. 10110
www.wwnorton.com

W. W. Norton & Company Ltd.
Castle House, 75/76 Wells Street, London W1T 3QT

1 2 3 4 5 6 7 8 9 0

For Barbara

Contents

Acknowledgments

The following poems have appeared or will appear
in these journals:

American Poetry Review: "The Insistence of Beauty,"
"In the Open Field"

Brilliant Corners: "Open Door Blues"

The Georgia Review: "Juarez," "Monogamy," "The Stories"

The Gettysburg Review: "The Answers," "The Answers,"
Cohabiting"

Hotel Amerika: "Beliefs," "The Stairway"

Iowa Review: "Five Roses in the Morning," "Getting Places"

The Kenyon Review: "Turning to the Page"

MARGIE: "In the Land of the Salamander," "The Waiting"

Poetry: "Dismantling the House," "The House Was Quiet,"
"Another Day," "From the Garden"

Tin House: "The Man," "For Many Years"

"Open Door Blues" was published in
The Best American Poetry 2003 (Scribner)

"Grudges" was published in *Poetry After 9/11*
(Melville House Press)
"Dismantling the House," "Monogamy," "Turning to the
Page," and "Achilles in Love" were published in *The Breath of
Parted Lips*, Vol. II: Poetry from the Robert Frost Place
(CavanKerry Press)

My special gratitude to Lawrence Raab whose brilliant and
scrupulous attention to drafts of these poems made every
single one of them better.

Thanks also to the MacDowell Colony for two residencies
where many of these poems found their beginnings.

And my great thanks to Carol Houck Smith, my editor,
for this, our ninth book together.

"It is always too late to argue with beauty . . .
Beauty isn't nice. Beauty isn't fair."

— PETER SCHJELDAHL

". . . and I could imagine that good cellist
angling his bow in such a way
as to name, then rename, a feeling."

— LINES FROM *"Something Loveless Out There"*

The Stairway

The architect wanted to build a stairway
and suspend it with silver, almost invisible
guy wires in a high-ceilinged room,
a stairway you couldn't ascend or descend
except in your dreams. But first—
because wild things are not easily seen
if what's around them is wild—
he'd make sure the house that housed it
was practical, built two-by-four by
two-by-four, slat by slat, without ornament.
The stairway would be an invitation
to anyone who felt invited by it,
and depending on your reaction he'd know
if friendship were possible.
The house he'd claim as his, but the stairway
would be designed to be ownerless,
tilted against any suggestion of a theology,
disappointing to those looking for politics.
Of course the architect knew
that over the years he'd have to build
other things the way others desired,

knew that to live in this world was to trade
a few industrious hours for one beautiful one.
Yet every night when he got home
he could imagine, as he walked in the door,
his stairway going nowhere, not for sale,
and maybe some you to whom nothing
about it need be explained, waiting,
the wine decanted, the night about to unfold.

I

Turning to the Page

I remember that cavernous silence
after my first declaration of love,
then, feeling I must have been
misunderstood, saying it again,

and, years later, with someone else,
exclaiming, "That was so good!"
and the foreign language she—who was
speaking English—used in response.

I learned there's nothing more shaming
or as memorable as an intimacy
unreturned. And turned, therefore,
to the expected silence of a page,

where I might simultaneously assert
and hide, be my own disappointment,
which saved me for a while.
But soon the page whispered

I'd mistaken its vastness for a refuge,
its whiteness for a hospital
for the pathetic. Fill me up, it said,
give me sorrow because I must have joy,

all the travails of love because
distances are where the safe reside.
Bring to me, it said, continual proof
you've been alive.

From the Garden

The flowers were sulking in their sensitive beds
as if they couldn't bear a moment without praise,

and the shadow boys were feeling undefined,
just a bunch of gray guys on a cold, gray day.

Elsewhere orchids in their hot, glass houses
smugly opened and preened, their privilege

the kind a shadow boy in his prime
might have addressed with a switchblade.

I was out among the slugs, watching them leave
their trademark traces of slime. From the garden

it seemed there wasn't a place I couldn't be,
a thing I couldn't imagine. What a good day,

I thought, for ugliness to have its revenge,
for worms to be given a corpse.

Once—before I learned what I wasn't—
I lingered on street corners

in my black and gold satin jacket,
a small-time innocent, looking for a grievance.

Now I wanted to go inside where it was lamplit,
warm, everything artificial and mine.

I took off my muddy shoes, turned the burner on
under the teapot, waited for it to call me

as if it were something hurt or wild. It did.
With just a touch, I made it subside.

Open Door Blues

The male wild turkey in the field
is all puffed up and unfurled.
Pecking at the ground, absorbed,
the female doesn't seem to care;
no sex, she seems to say,
before food. He looks the fool.
Cool air since you've been gone.
I haven't touched the heat, yet
the baseboard heaters are pinging
an atonal song. Balanced on its
haunches, your rocking chair
isn't rocking anymore. It can't,
alone, be fully what it is. I've
given it every one of its thoughts.
It thinks you'll not return.
The creature that's burrowed
inside the wall, probably a squirrel,
is chewing something with bones.
Every time I kick the spot,
it stops, but not for long.

It seems to believe it can't be hurt.
I've left the door open. The flies
know. The wasps soon will.

For Many Years

Some nights I had to go there,
where I could not dare to stay.

No white dividing line made it clear
which side of the road was mine,

and when I parked and got out
no moon streaked a path.

I knew the way *by heart.*
That was the kind I had.

I'd give the equivalent of a sop
to Cerberus, and walk right in.

Ruin, with whom I'd come to flirt,
as usual was looking good.

I just needed to smell her perfume,
spend a little time under her spell.

Never was it easy getting back.
You can't trust a heart,

its attachments to the new,
how quickly it forgets its way.

The dog would awaken and bark.
And the story of how I got lost

in the navigable dark
each time needed to feel true.

The Stories

FOR M.A.W.

(1939 – 1994)

I was unfaithful to you last week.
Though I tried to be true
to the beautiful vagaries
of our unauthorized love,
I told a stranger our story,
arranging and rearranging us
until we were orderly, reduced.
I didn't want to sleep with this stranger.
I wanted, I think, to see her yield,
to sense her body's musculature,
her history of sane resistance
become pliable, as yours had
twenty-two years ago.
I told her we met in parks
and rest stops along highways.
Once, deep in the woods,
a blanket over stones and dirt.
I said that you were, finally,
my failure of nerve,
made to the contours of my body,

so wrongly good for me
I had to give you up.
Listening to myself, it seemed
as if I were still inconsolable,
and I knew the seductiveness in that,
knew when she'd try to console me
I'd allow her the tiniest of victories.
I told her about Laguna, the ruins
we made of each other.
To be undone—I said I learned
that's what I'd always wanted.
We were on a train from Boston
to New York, this stranger and I,
the compartment to ourselves.
I don't have to point out to you
the erotics of such a space.
We'd been speaking of our marriages,
the odd triumphs of their durations.
"Once . . . ," I said, and my betrayal began,
and did not end.
She had a story, too.

Mine seemed to coax hers out.
There was this man she'd meet
every workday Thursday at noon.
For three years, every Thursday
except Thanksgiving. She couldn't
bear it anymore, she said,
the lies, the coming home.
Ended, she said.
Happiest years of her life, she said.
At that moment (you understand)
we had to hug, but that's all we did.
It hardly matters. We were in each other's
sanctums, among the keepsakes,
we'd gone where most sex cannot go.
I could say that telling her our story
was a way of bringing you back to life,
and for a while it was, a memorial
made of memory and its words.
But here's what I knew:
Watching her react, I was sure I'd tell
our story again, to others. I understood

how it could be taken to the bank,
and I feared I might not ever again
feel enough to know when to stop.

The House Was Quiet

After Stevens

The house was quiet and the world vicious,
peopled as it is with those deprived
of this or that necessity, and with weasels, too,
and brutes, who don't even need
a good excuse. The house was quiet as if it knew
it had been split. There was a sullenness
in its quiet. A hurt. The house was us.
It wasn't a vicious house, not yet. We hadn't
yet denuded its walls, rolled up its rugs.
It had no knowledge of the world
and thus of those who, in the name of justice,
would ransack belongings, cut throats.
Once the house had resounded with stories.
Now it was quiet, it was terrible how quiet it was.
And, sensing an advantage, the world pressed in.

Dismantling the House

Rent a flatbed with a winch.
With the right leverage
anything can be hoisted, driven off.

Or the man with a Bobcat comes in,
then the hauler with his enormous truck.
A leveler or a lawyer does the rest;

experts always are willing to help
The structure was old, rotten in spots.
Hadn't it already begun to implode?

Believe you've just sped the process up.
Photographs, toys, the things that break
your heart—let's trust

they would have been removed,
perhaps are safe with the children
who soon will have children of their own.

It's over. It's time for loss to build
its tower in the yard where you
are merely a spectator now.

Admit you'd like to find something
discarded or damaged, even gone,
and lift it back into the world.

Love-Lies-Bleeding

I said to her who takes plants seriously,

Someone gave Love-Lies-Bleeding its name,
who on a different day, differently reminded,
might have called it Love's Sweet Aftermath
or Early Passion, its drooping purple-red
flowering spikes so broadly suggestive.

We had the book open between us.

That someone, I continued, must have been
an authority for the name to have stuck.
Don't you think so? Or perhaps a wit.

Isn't Love-Lies-Bleeding comic,
like midlife crises to those long past them?
The name, I mean, isn't it funny,
like B movies, the dialogue purple
as a giant bruise, all the characters
actually saying out loud what they think?

No, I don't think it's funny, not at all,
she said, and laughed the way I'd seen
good actors do in lieu of what they felt.
It was time to stop talking about it, I was sure.

But I continued on.

Juarez

FOR L.

What sad freedom I have,
now that we're unwed.
I can tell the Juarez story,
which you wouldn't let me tell,
though I assured you
I'd tell it as evidence
of the strange places the soul
hides, and why I fell in love.
It was yours, you said. You
wouldn't let me make it mine.
You were in El Paso, a flight
attendant. Between jobs?
I can't quite remember. Men
gravitated to you as if they were
falling apples and you the earth.
This man you were dating, your
El Paso guy, as you called him,
said he knew a whorehouse
in Juarez, a place where
the whores danced and you could
get a table, have drinks, watch.

Let's go, he said, and you did,
with another couple,
parking your car on the U.S. side,
walking in. It was 1961.
You were adventuresome, young.
You didn't know the verb, *to slum*.
You passed an excavation site,
then some adobe shacks, children
barefoot and begging. You passed
a man on a burro. And soon
you were a turista amid the dismal
liveliness of a border town.
Your date was handsome, high-
spirited. You weren't yet sure
if he mattered to you.
The dancing whores had holes
in their underwear. One couldn't
have been more than fifteen.
They danced badly, as if bad
was what everyone wanted—
herky-jerky, lewd. Your date

was clapping. (I remember the face
you made as you said this.)
On the way back, he spoke of the fun
he'd had. Off to your right was
the excavation site.
You didn't know why,
but you climbed down into it as far
as you could go, sat curled up facing
cement blocks, the beginnings
of a foundation. Your friends thought
you a wild woman, a jokester.
But you didn't say anything.
And you wouldn't come up.
For the longest time you wouldn't
come up. Even when they went down
to get you, you wouldn't come up.
I'm sorry. If you hadn't stopped me
I'd have been telling this
over and over for years.
By now, you'd have corrected
the errors of timing, errors of fact.

It would be that much more yours.
Or maybe you knew that a story
always belongs to its teller,
that nothing you could have said—
once it was told in my voice—
would much matter. Perhaps.
But, after all, it's my story too.
On that dark Juarez night,
every step of your troubled descent
was toward me. I was waiting
in the future for such a woman.

Good Dinners

Despair is perfectly compatible
with a good dinner, I promise you.
— WILLIAM M. THACKERAY

I loved your risotto, your coq au vin,
the care you gave everything you prepared.
I loved even your meat loafs and stews.
You, of course, couldn't love
what you'd done; the true maker never can.
Those arrangements on the plate: still lifes
designed to disappear.
In a certain mood, one could say you provided
experiences that foreshadowed loss.
Too cruel, I know, but you made me want more,
and I consumed and withheld.
Rumaki, stuffed grape leaves, I praised
the talents you were sure of—
what almost no one yearns to hear.
You kept track—x's next to things
you thought we wouldn't want again.
I was always present, always somewhere else.
No wonder I didn't realize until now
how much despair must have been yours.

The Past

Herrings begin to glow just after they die,
never while alive. When I read this
I wanted to sit for a long time in the dark.
Nothing in nature is a metaphor.
Everything is. I thought both thoughts.
And knew inexactly why I felt sad.
Herrings dead and aglow—
I should have been properly amazed,
the way anyone looking at a star
would be, realizing it was years away,
untouchable. Yet there it is, shining.

Grudges

Easy for almost anything to occur.
Even if we've scraped the sky, we can be rubble.
For years those men felt one way, acted another.

Ground zero, is it possible to get lower?
Now we had a new definition of the personal,
knew almost anything could occur.

It just takes a little training to blur
a motive, lie low while planning the terrible,
get good at acting one way, feeling another.

Yet who among us doesn't harbor
a grudge or secret? So much isn't erasable;
it follows that almost anything can occur,

like men ascending into the democracy of air
without intending to land, the useful veil
of having said one thing, meaning another.

Before you know it something's over.
Suddenly someone's missing at the table.
It's easy (I know it) for anything to occur
when men feel one way, act another.

The Answers

After Mark Strand

Why did you leave me?

We had grown tired together. Don't you remember?
We'd grown tired together, were going through the motions.

Why did you leave me?

I don't know, really. There was comfort in that tiredness.
There was love,

Why did you leave me?

You began to correct my embellishments in public.
You wouldn't let me tell my stories.

Why did you leave me?

She is . . . I don't wish to be
any more cruel than I've been.

You son-of-a-bitch.

Why did you leave me?

I was already gone.
I just brought my body with me.

Why did you leave me?

You found out and I found I couldn't give her up.
I was as shocked as you were.

Why didn't you lie to me?

I was already lying to you. It was hard work.
All of it suddenly felt like hard work.

Why did you leave me?

I wanted to try monogamy again.
I wanted the freedom to be monogamous.

You fucker. You fucking son-of-a-bitch.

Why did you leave me?

I wanted you both. I thought I could be faithful
to each of you. You shouldn't have made me choose.

Don't you know what betrayal is?

I never thought of it as betrayal. More like one pleasure
of mine you should never have known.

You are really quite an awful man.

Why did you leave me?

It was time to leave.
The hour of leaving had come.

Why did you leave me?

It would take too long to explain. Please
don't ask me to explain.

Will you not explain it to me?

No, I will not explain it to you. I'll say anything
rather than explain it to you. Even things that sound true.

II

Another Day

Last night a succubus-bitten moon followed me all the way
    home,
and on the tape was a message from my friend, the mathe-
    matician,
wanting to know if I thought an apple was as elegant as a
    circle.
I found it impossible to muster any original response, not
    even
a funny one, and slept poorly, and dreamt of Brando in
    Streetcar
and, as the mind would have it, of a torturer in Pinochet's
    Chile,
after a hard day's work, bringing groceries home to his family.

Nothing was much better or, really, much worse, when I
    woke.
I wasn't thinking of possums and prairie dogs and all the sly
little things of the world peeping out of their holes, or
    mustangs
in Wyoming snorting in a canyon after a long run—nothing
so sweet—but of someone religious who's never had a crisis

of faith, and therefore can't be trusted. It meant I was ready to
    write
another version of what I'd written before, and why not?
    Maybe
I could ransack Schopenhauer this time. Maybe slightly alter
Augustine. Do I drift and tamper because no landscape
keeps and grounds me? Not one lascivious city. Not the most
verdant valley. I must have two souls, the empty one that
    aches
to be filled, and a dull, fat one. I called my friend, and said
    "Yes."

When it became clear I wasn't ready to do anything but drift,
it looked like another day of *if* and *I wish,* another day
in the subjunctive, and there I was, once again waiting
for something to present itself. After his car accident,
the mathematician was told he had a bruised heart
and a cracked sternum. Would he live any differently
when he got better? someone asked. "Yes," he said,
and here's why we're friends: he couldn't think

of a single way. Maybe it's the comfort of postponements
that I fear, life as rehearsal for a life. After oblivion . . . bliss,
once declared the saddest person I've ever known.

III

The Waiting

I waited for you calmly, with infinite patience.
I waited for you hungrily, just short of desperate.

When you came I knew that desperate was unattractive.
I was calm, no one wants the kind of calm I was.

It tried your patience, it made you hungry for a man
who was hungry. I am that man, I said,

but I said it calmly. My body was an ache, a silence.
It could not affirm how long it had waited for you.

It could not claw or insist or extend its hands.
It was just a stupid body, closed up and voracious.

Beliefs

I believed in nothing, so I thought
no system of smoke and desire
got in the way of what I saw.

There was the other world
if only it could be seen,
slag heaps and golden valleys,
crime and celibacy—

visible companions—if, say,
your politics could braid them,
and there were all the gods
in the darkness of our needs.

That was when I realized
that to believe in nothing
is a belief too, and not much fun
either, and acceptance

of the world as it is is as dumb
as standing still when floodwaters rise.
Fortunately in the midst of it all

you came along with your singular beauty,
the truth of things for a while
tactile and unequivocal.

But often when you left the room
a few questions replaced you.
When you returned, they remained.

Is it possible to be in love
and wise at the same time?

In love, I might be so intuitively right
I'd be banned from a republic. In love
I might believe any foolish thing I felt.

Over time, questions formed curlicues
in your hair. They became part of what
I thought when I thought about you.

So good, then, when you stayed in the room,
giving them flesh, making them real.

Something Loveless Out There

Last night—like any night filled with music
and love's ever-doubling entendres—
last night felt intrinsically naughty and ripe
for admonishment, but we'd made it our business
to stay apart from the admonishers and their nays.
We'd already made naughty nice,
and the indifferent world, for us, a better place.
The music recalled in me a sadness
without which I know I couldn't know
what I had, and I could imagine that good cellist
angling his bow in such a way
as to name, then rename, a feeling.
For a while it didn't matter that the promised
ice storm had arrived. We got into bed
and listened to the sharp sounds
that signaled the tops of birches and oak
descending in the dark, each crack evidence
some intolerable limit had been reached.
Oh it had nothing to do with us.
Yet our bodies became differently alert,
as if aware of something loveless out there,

worse than an admonisher, not one soft spot.
Come morning power lines were down,
everything crusted and slick, the driveway
impassable. But there we were, alive, unhurt,
and I remember how in silence, not awe,
we noted destruction's strange beauty,
determined to give it nothing more than respect.

Cohabiting

There's not a nude in a museum
or a person anywhere, taking a bath,
nearly as naked as that French girl,
stripped of all but her socks,
head shaved, being spat upon
by her own townspeople
in one of history's sunlit
cobblestone squares. I've only
read about her, but somehow,
for me, she's permanently fixed,
a scaffolding of awful
yet understandable righteousness
surrounding her, accentuating
the stark paleness of her skin,
the big war finally over,
and behind it, for centuries,
those without pity
with their saliva and their stones.

I imagine how it began
between them, a man in a uniform
she had to have been wary of,
a man, in fact, dressed to kill,
touching her in some exactly
right place in a wrong time.
And I see her resisting for as long
as she can—minutes, weeks—
her mind searching for principles
her body doesn't seem to have.
Perhaps she thinks it's the end
of her world, what has she to lose?
Or she just falls
into those irrevocable tomorrows
like someone who knows
only what she feels, the enemy slowly
transformed into a man as lonely
as she is, with beautiful hands.

I can see the picture clearly now.
Terrified, she rushes forward,
which makes no sense, but I remember
when I did the same. Everything
in my education said, no, go back,
and I went headlong into the flames.

Monogamy

Start again, try to say it
with a little brio this time, a dash
of wasabi in the first sentence,
some paprika perhaps
for the sake of p's, and turn loose
the drummer in you
(your best-kept secret) who loves
the intermittent, yet heart-timed
clack of drumstick against metal.

After all, there's the suddenly desirable
mono in monogamy to celebrate,
the new freedom of wanting
only one person. Start again,
but admit you wouldn't advocate this
for anyone save yourself. Acknowledge
it's a state you've traveled far
to reach, motels and the overly careful
spelling of aliases behind you.
Acknowledge it takes long experience

in order to think of sameness
as an opportunity for imagination.

Call yourself a monk and call her
a nun, and remember the fun of words
lying down with other words.
Think syntax. Think combos
and ménages, it's all right, my friend,
to include the various in the one.
You're in love. It's springtime. Birds
are making a racket in a thousand thickets.

Achilles in Love

There was no getting to his weakness.
In public, even in summer, he wore
big boots, specially made for him,
a band of steel reinforcing each heel.
At home, when he bathed or slept,
he kept a pistol within reach, loaded.
And because to be invulnerable
is to be alone, he was alone even when
he was with you. You could sense it
in the rigidity of his carriage, as if under
his fine-fitting suits were layers of armor.
Yet everyone loved to see him in action:
While his enemies were thinking of small
advantages, he only thought end game.

Then she came along, who seemed to be all
women fused into one, cheekbones and breasts
evidence that evolution doesn't care
about fairness, and a mind so good, well,
it was like his. You could see his body soften,
and days later, when finally they were naked,

she instinctively knew what to do—
as smart men do with a mastectomy's scar—
kiss his heel before kissing
what he considered to be his power,
and with a tenderness that made him tremble.

And so Achilles began to live differently.
Both friends and enemies were astounded
by his willingness to listen, and hesitate
before responding. Even in victory he'd
walk away without angering a single god.
He wore sandals now because she liked him in sandals.
He never felt so exposed, or so open to the world.
You could see in his face something resembling terror,
but in fact it was love, for which he would die.

In the Open Field

That man in the field staring at the sky
without the excuse of a dog
or rifle—there must be a reason
why I've put him there.
Only moments ago, he didn't exist.
He might be claiming this field
as his own, centering himself in it
until confident he belongs. Or
he could be dangerous, one of those
men who doesn't know
why he talks to God.
I thought of making him a flamingo
standing alone on one pink leg,
a symbol of discordancy
between object and environment.
But I've grown so weary of inventions
that startle but don't satisfy.
I think he must have come to grieve
a good friend's death, and just wants
to stand there, numbly, quite sure
the sky he's looking at is vacant.

But I see that he may be smiling—
his friend's death was years ago—
and he might be out there to savor
the solitary elation of having discovered
what had eluded him until now.

Anniversary of the Rain and the Rule

It was raining, and you blamed our lovemaking
on your weakness for how a downpour sounds
as if you didn't know the body unrules,
hand-feeds the mind the reasons it needs.

This morning the rain again is arguing
some good, vague case for whatever
we might be feeling, but from our bed
what brings me back to that afternoon

when you slipped, in all senses, into my life
isn't rain's permission but the speeding cars
sizzling on wet asphalt.
Because we don't know who's driving them,

or where, if anyplace, they're going.
Because we can't know, yet it seems
something's burning as they pass.
The rule? You'd do this, but not that—

your bargain with the illicit, or was it
with some devil in yourself?
Love laughs at locksmiths, the saying goes.
And it had begun to rain.

You were helpless, is what you claimed.
And now the anniversary of that day
in which you came round has come around.
Not a single car is slowing down.

Getting Places

That red gash in the hills, I told her,
is bauxite, not clay. I saw that it was *gash*
that made her smile. What about
those cows the color of Irish Setters
grazing in the lowland? she asked.
Oh, just big, slow dogs.
Thank you, she replied, like Elvis,
thank you very much.
That over there, I said, feeling it now,
is bougainvillea, and see, up the trail,
that house, the one gutted by fire?
It once belonged to a famous bandit
and his high-maintenance woman,
dear friends of mine.
I like the word *cornucopia,* she said,
the sound and size of it,
that's the kind of girl I am.
I understand, I didn't say.
Instead I told her that beyond
the red gash in the hills
are the caves, and beyond the caves

are the monasteries beyond sleep
where you get to lie down.
Good, she said, we're getting places now.

In the Land of the Salamander

Salamander land, we called that island
where we'd gone to do damage to our routines.
And the fourteen kinds of loneliness we'd named

one night when we felt close enough to dare—
we'd do some damage to them too.
In the land of the salamander, pleasure is king.

Each day in your Speedo you snorkeled
amid bright fish, and reefs of coral so beautiful
if you touched them they'd rip your hand.

I followed in the clear blue, feeling like what I was—
a masked man with big flippers, silly, not quite
buoyant, not nearly the sleek natural you were.

When we returned to shore, you allowed me
to speak of barracudas and bananafish, knowing
I loved words more than anything I might have seen.

And back in our room, I mapped with my tongue
the reddish line where your swimsuit ended
and skin began, claiming certain territory as mine.

Any way a loneliness can be subtracted,
we decided, is a lovely thing.

Meanwhile the islanders secretly seethed.
We could feel it in their niceness, in every
Sir and Madam, it was there behind their eyes.

But we had years of experience in forgetting
what we felt. We told ourselves they were beautiful
as coral, that their English was song.

After all, we'd traveled so long and come so far
to where salamanders abound and pleasure's
a commodity. We'd come with baggage

we were willing to pay others to carry awhile.

The salamanders were green, sometimes red,

and whenever we came close to them they blended in.

The Man

In bed after love she tells you
about a man in her life, a wrong man
who introduced her
when she was very young
to the forbidden, to the radiant life
of the secret. She's speaking of him
with such fondness
you know this is where she began
to become the person she is today,
and you're grateful to this man,
in fact you know he's in bed with you,
and that next time, for her sake,
you'll try to be both him and yourself.
With your new-found tenderness
you'll press into her doubly hard.
This you will keep from her,
even after she cries out only your name.

Five Roses in the Morning

MARCH 16, 2003

On TV the showbiz of war,
so I turn it off
wishing I could turn it off,
and glance at the five white roses
in front of the mirror on the mantel,
looking like ten.
That they were purchased out of love
and are not bloody red
won't change a goddamned thing —
goddamned things, it seems, multiplying
every day. Last night
the roses numbered six, but she chose
to wear one in her hair,
and she was more beautiful
because she believed she was.
It changed the night a little.
For us, I mean.

Cruelties

When Peter Lorre, Casablanca's pathetic, good-hearted man,
said, "You despise me, don't you?" and Bogart replied,
"Well, if I gave you any thought, I might,"

I laughed, which the movie permitted.
It had all of us leaning Bogart's way.

"Nothing is funnier than unhappiness," Beckett has one
of his characters say, as if it might be best
to invent others to speak certain things
we've thought and kept to ourselves.

If any of us, real or fictional, had said to someone,
"Nothing's funnier than your unhappiness,"
we'd have entered another, colder realm,

like when news came that a famous writer had died
in an accident, and his rival said,
"I guess that proves God can read."
Many of us around him laughed.
Then a dark, uneasy silence set in.

All day long, my former love, I've been revising
a poem about us. First, a gentle man
spoke it, then I gave the Devil a chance.
But you always knew my someone else
could only be me.

The Answers

Won't you speak to me?

No, it would remind me
of what I haven't said.

But I need to speak to you.

I know what you need,
and your needs don't matter now.
Go talk to her about your needs.

What if I said please?

I am unreachable.
If I were standing next to you
you'd see for yourself
how far away I was.

I'll speak for you then.

Go ahead. Fine. Once again
you'll be talking to yourself.

Do you think that, maybe, over time . . . ?

There aren't enough years.

How can you be so sure?

I feel what I feel.

And is there no complicity in what you feel?
Remember, you were no saint.

There are some questions that are obscene.
There are some questions that one loses the right to ask.

I'd like to speak to you.

But I will not speak to you,
and have not spoken to you.
Admit it, and tell everyone:
Despite appearances,
I haven't said a single word.

Sleeping with Others

Because memory and its intrusive nostalgias
    lie down with us,
it helps to say we love each other,

each declaration a small erasure, the past
    for a while reduced to a trace,
the heart's palimpsest to a murmur.

Still, our solitudes are so populated
    that sometimes after sex
we know it's best to be quiet—

time having instructed us in the art
    of the unspoken,
or in the sufficient eloquence

of certain sighs. Regret shows up
    unpredictably,
sleeping with, but never between us.

Like joy it doesn't stay long, quickly tiring
    of the language
used in its name, wanting only itself.

We've made this bed. We're old enough
    to know sorrow may visit
now and then, and that the world slides in

at will—ugly, dark, confident it belongs.
    Nothing to do but let it
touch us, allow it to hurt, and remind.

The Insistence of Beauty

The day before those silver planes
came out of the perfect blue, I was struck
by the beauty of pollution rising
from smokestacks near Newark,
gray and white ribbons of it
on their way to evanescence.

And at impact, no doubt, certain beholders
and believers from another part of the world
must have seen what appeared gorgeous—
the flames of something theirs being born.

I watched for hours—mesmerized—
that willful collision replayed,
the better man in me not yielding,
then yielding to revenge's sweet surge.

The next day there was a photograph
of dust and smoke ghosting a street,
and another of a man you couldn't be sure
was fear-frozen or dead or made of stone,

and for a while I was pleased
to admire the intensity—or was it the coldness?—
of each photographer's good eye.
For years I'd taken pride in resisting

the obvious—sunsets, snowy peaks,
a starlet's face—yet had come to realize
even those, seen just right, can have
their edgy place. And the sentimental,

beauty's sloppy cousin, that enemy,
can't it have a place too?
Doesn't a tear deserve a close-up?
When word came of a fireman

who hid in the rubble
so his dispirited search dog
could have someone to find, I repeated it
to everyone I knew. I did this for myself,
not for community or beauty's sake,
yet soon it had a rhythm and a frame.

Winter

Indifference of a perfect sky, and here, below,
the snowy residue of last week's storm
combine to form what not long ago
I might have called desire's *tabula rasa*,
or, in another mood, just nothingness.
Now they seem little more than what they are.
And those deer prints in the driveway,
that cardinal on a hemlock's lower branch—
I'm amazed they don't insist or signify.
Nor does the day seem to be waiting,
as once it did, for what I'd say and do.
There are clarities: the wind isn't my wind;
its whispers are everyone's intimacy. And
the neighbor's snowman, especially if given
a pipe and hat, soon will take on a sadness.
I walk my property without pride,
knowing it's mere morning here
when it's night in many an elsewhere,
or war, everywhere a commingling
of the beautiful and the treacherous.
I'd make a plan if I didn't know

there's something in the universe
that dislikes a plan. Nothing personal,
I've come to believe. Four starlings
on a telephone wire, an oak's bare branches—
no, not architecture, only a kind of evidence.